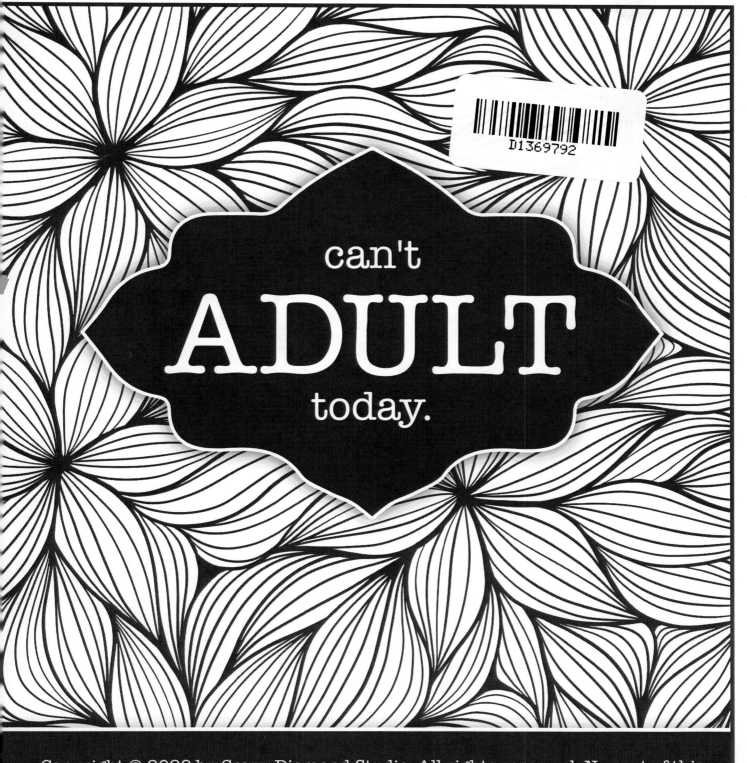

can't
ADULT
today.

Hello!

I'm Jami of Crazy Diamond Studio and this is my first coloring book! I'm an illustrator and graphic designer as well as a wife and mama living in Asheville, NC. Children's llustration is my passion, but trying new things makes me happy (like creating a coloring book for adults). Kick back, take some time out from the mundane tasks of adulting and color your sweet little heart out.

Tell life to flock off and just relax... Carpe Diem, Bitches!

Follow me on Etsy to see my other work and to keep up with my newest endeavors:

www.crazydiamondstudio.etsy.com

Dedication.

To all of you who have supported my many creative ventures along the way, thank you. And to all of you new supporters that decided to purchase this coloring book, thank you, too! Supporting independent artists like myself really puts the icing on the cake.

Coloring Tips.

From teens to your sweet ol' grandma... this book was created for a wide array of mature colorists with a sense of humor. "Can't Adult Today" offers detailed illustrations, but not so much that it makes you bat-shit crazy. This book is perfect for color pencils, fine tip pens, markers, crayons & more. Use the color test pages in the back of the book to test your mediums, colors and shading before putting them on your page.

Let your inspiration flow and enjoy!

mimosas it is.

Color Test Page

Color Test Page

Made in United States
North Haven, CT
26 May 2023

36999131R00030